HORRIBLE THINGS

Sick, Nasty Medical Practices

by Kelly Regan Barnhill

Consultant:
David D. Gilmore
Professor of Anthropology
Stony Brook University
Stony Brook, New York

Capstone
press®

Mankato, Minnesota

Edge Books are published by Capstone Press,
151 Good Counsel Drive, P.O. Box 669, Mankato, Minnesota 56002.
www.capstonepress.com

Library of Congress Cataloging-in-Publication Data
Barnhill, Kelly Regan.
    Sick, nasty medical practices / by Kelly Regan Barnhill.
    p. cm. — (Edge books. Horrible things)
    Includes bibliographical references and index.
    Summary: "Describes a variety of strange medical practices from the
past" — Provided by publisher.
    ISBN-13: 978-1-4296-2293-6 (hardcover)
    ISBN-10: 1-4296-2293-8 (hardcover)
    1. Medicine — History — Juvenile literature. 2. Medical innovations —
History — Juvenile literature. I. Title.
R133.5.B37 2009
610 — dc22   2008028706

Editorial Credits
Aaron Sautter, editor; Ted Williams, designer; Jo Miller, photo researcher

Photo Credits
Alamy/INTERFOTO/Pressebildagentur, 6; Nathan Benn, 13;
    Pictorial Press Ltd, 9; Scott Kemper, 29
AP Images/Frank Hormann, 10
Capstone Press/Karon Dubke, 4
Corbis/Bettmann, 18; Swim Ink 2 LLC, 14
Digger Odell, 27
From "Medicine: Perspectives in History and Art", Courtesy of
    Robert E. Greenspan, MD, 24
Getty Images Inc./Hulton Archive, 26; National Geographic/
    Jason Edwards, 8
The Granger Collection, New York, 17, 20, 25
The Image Works/Topham/AAAC, 12
Newscom, 16 (bottle); Getty Images/Hulton Archive, 15; San Jose
    Mercury News/Judith Calson, 19
Photo Researchers, Inc/Science Photo Library, 23
Shutterstock/Andraz Cerar, 16 (mercury drops)
Visuals Unlimited/Dr. Fred Hossler, cover

2 3 4 5 6 14 13 12 11 10 09

Table of Contents

Dangerous Medicine

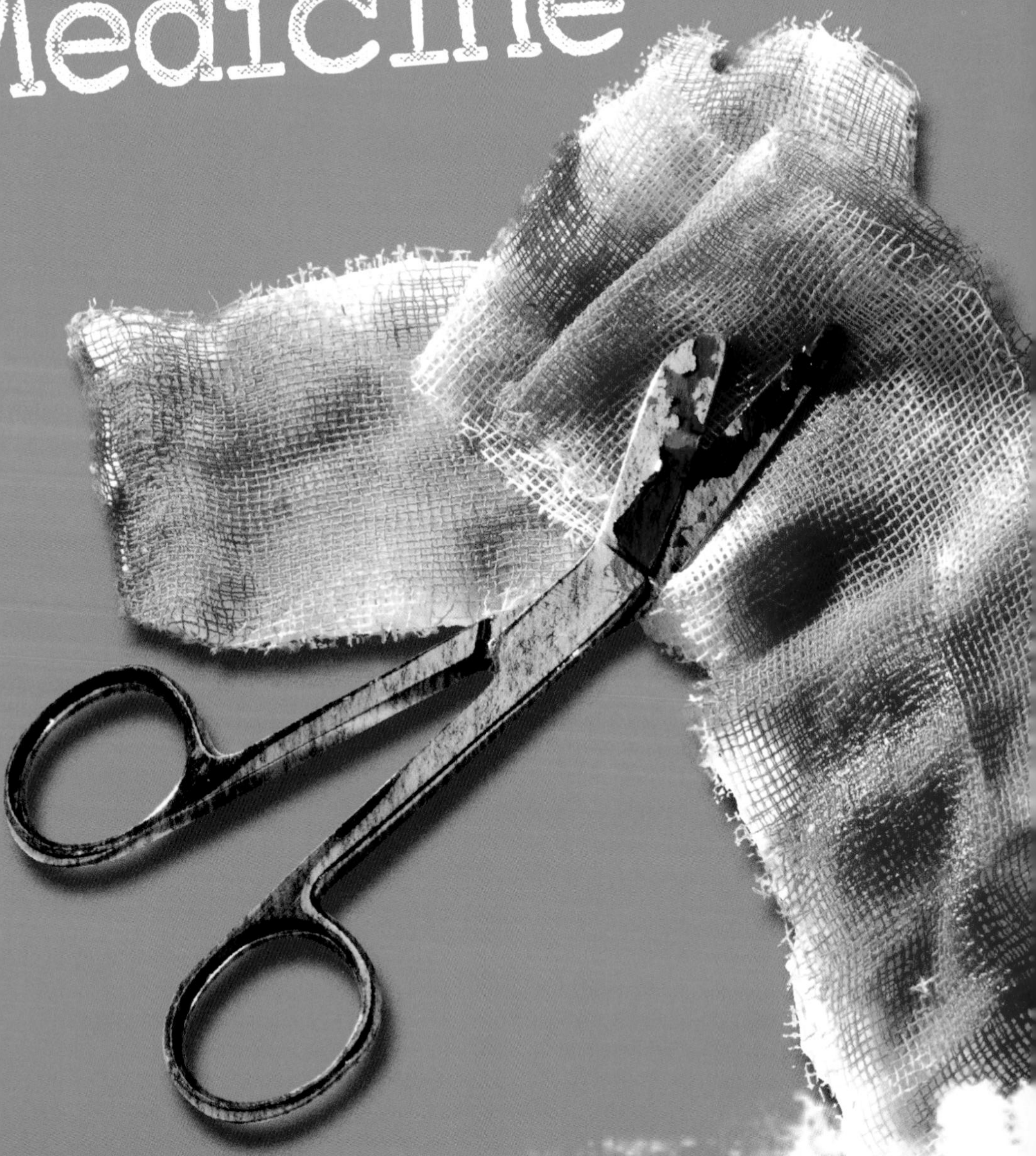

For many people, a trip to the doctor is a horrible experience. The smell of the doctor's office sickens them. Long, sharp needles can be terrifying. They're scared stiff when the doctor looms over them.

Fortunately, the doctor's office is really a safe place. Modern medicine improves every year. Most doctors are kind, smart people who care about their patients.

Long ago, however, medicine was a dangerous business. Little was understood about the human body. Doctors caused patients to die almost as often as they healed them. Let's take a look at medicine's darker past.

1

Bloodletting

Doctors once believed that patients could be healed by removing excess blood.

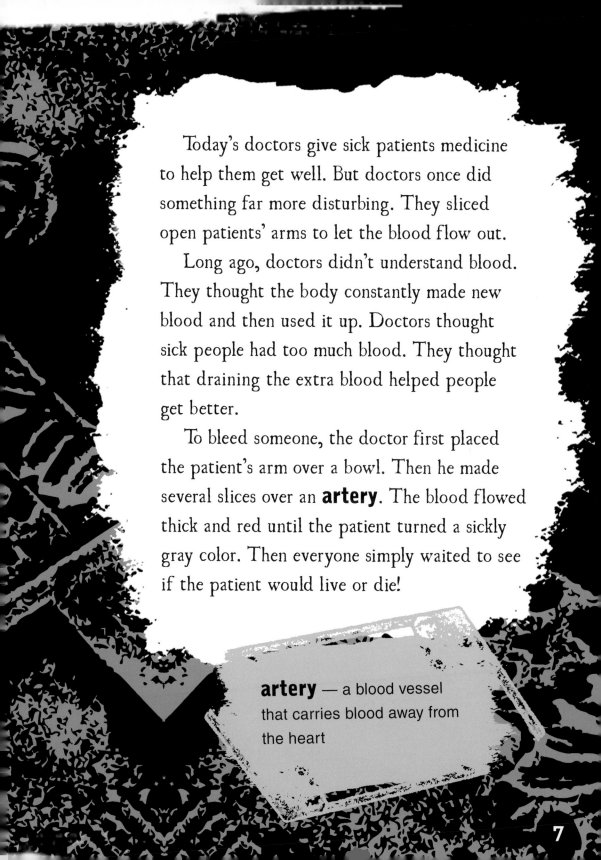

Today's doctors give sick patients medicine to help them get well. But doctors once did something far more disturbing. They sliced open patients' arms to let the blood flow out.

Long ago, doctors didn't understand blood. They thought the body constantly made new blood and then used it up. Doctors thought sick people had too much blood. They thought that draining the extra blood helped people get better.

To bleed someone, the doctor first placed the patient's arm over a bowl. Then he made several slices over an **artery**. The blood flowed thick and red until the patient turned a sickly gray color. Then everyone simply waited to see if the patient would live or die!

artery — a blood vessel that carries blood away from the heart

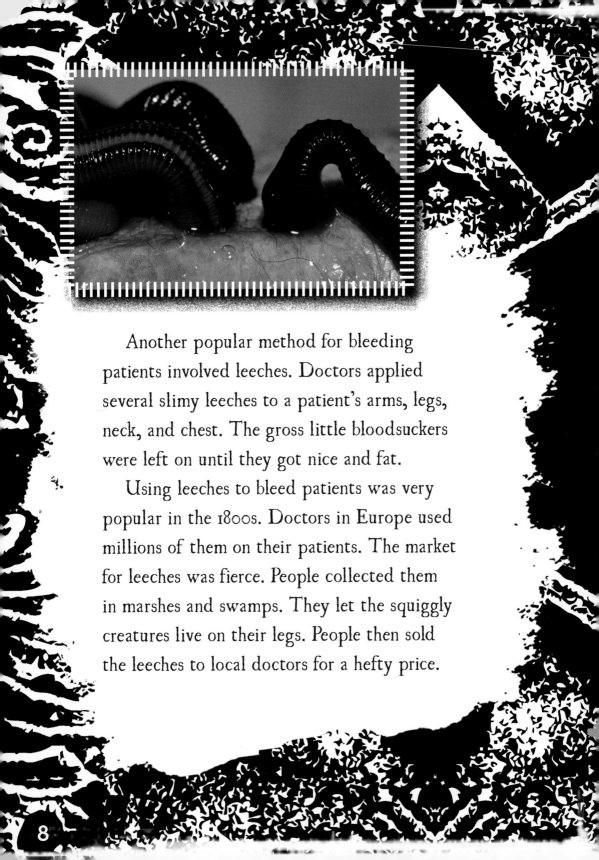

Another popular method for bleeding patients involved leeches. Doctors applied several slimy leeches to a patient's arms, legs, neck, and chest. The gross little bloodsuckers were left on until they got nice and fat.

Using leeches to bleed patients was very popular in the 1800s. Doctors in Europe used millions of them on their patients. The market for leeches was fierce. People collected them in marshes and swamps. They let the squiggly creatures live on their legs. People then sold the leeches to local doctors for a hefty price.

DEATH OF A PRESIDENT

One famous example of bleeding a patient involved U.S. President George Washington. One cold December day in 1799, Washington was suffering from a nasty throat infection. His doctors decided to remove almost 1 gallon (4 liters) of his blood. The loss of blood made Washington so weak that he died within a few hours.

Trepanation

Ancient priests may have drilled holes in people's skulls to get rid of evil spirits.

What would you do for a terrible headache in the Middle Ages? Drill a hole in your head, of course! At least, that's what many people did at the time. It was called trepanation, and it was extremely dangerous.

HORRIBLE FACT

Archaeologists have found skulls dating back to 10,000 BC with trepanation holes in them. Several cave paintings also show people going through the process.

Back then, this operation was used to cure everything from headaches to mental illness. Doctors used crude tools and had nothing to kill germs or reduce pain. They had to be extremely careful. One wrong move, and they could kill their patients. People who survived often suffered from brain damage or serious infections.

PSYCHIC HOLES IN THE HEAD

A few people still practice trepanation. These people believe it makes them telepathic, or able to read minds. They think the holes in their skulls help them pick up psychic energy waves.

Today, people use better tools and cleaner locations to perform the operation. Patients are also given lots of painkillers. Do holes in people's skulls actually help them read minds? It's very unlikely. There's no scientific evidence to support the claim.

Staying Filthy

The Black Plague killed millions of people in the Middle Ages.

The Black Plague was a horrible disease in the mid-1300s. Symptoms included high fevers and aching joints. Victims also had swollen glands that oozed pus and dark blood. People in Europe died by the thousands.

Back then, people believed diseases were evil vapors that entered through the skin. They thought a thick layer of sweat and dirt would help keep them healthy. So they stopped bathing. But smelly bodies didn't offer any protection. By 1400, the Black Plague had killed nearly half of Europe's population.

HORRIBLE FACT

Doctors commonly bled people who had the Black Plague. When the doctor cut a patient's arms, the blood oozed out thick and dark. And it was usually mixed with foul-smelling pus.

BATHING BEHAVIOR

In the 1500s, England's Queen Elizabeth I tried to get people to bathe more often. She said that she took a bath at least once a month whether she needed it or not.

This was shocking news for many people of the time. Most people took baths only a few times a year. Bathing was a lot of hard work. First, water had to be carried to the bathhouse. Then it had to be heated. People burned wood to heat the water. So lots of wood had to be carried to the bathhouse too. Most people couldn't afford the cost of bathing regularly.

Mrs. Winslow's Soothing Syrup

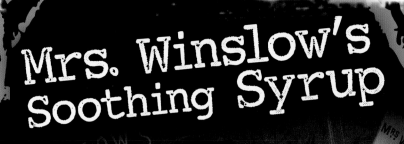

Parents sometimes gave kids fake medicine so they would fall asleep faster.

In the late 1800s, terrible sicknesses were everywhere. Parents constantly worried about how to care for sick children. When their kids got sick, parents often turned to new medicines.

Many parents chose Mrs. Winslow's Soothing Syrup for their kids. They didn't know that one of the main ingredients was morphine. This drug is now known to cause **addiction** and even death. The syrup helped kids feel better for a while. But it also caused kids to become addicted. Some kids even died when they drank too much of it.

addiction — a dependence on a drug or other substance

ART IMITATES LIFE

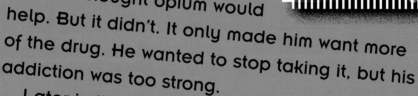

Famous writer Robert Louis Stevenson was addicted to opium as a child. He had asthma, a condition that affected his breathing. Doctors thought opium would help. But it didn't. It only made him want more of the drug. He wanted to stop taking it, but his addiction was too strong.

Later in life, Stevenson wrote a book called *Dr. Jekyll and Mr. Hyde*. It's about a man who took a potion that turned him into an evil creature. In the book, Dr. Jekyll becomes addicted to the potion. Many people believe the story is based on Stevenson's own drug addiction.

HORRIBLE FACT

During the late 1800s, people used many fake tonics and syrups. They didn't know the fake medicines contained addictive drugs like heroine, cocaine, and opium.

Mercury

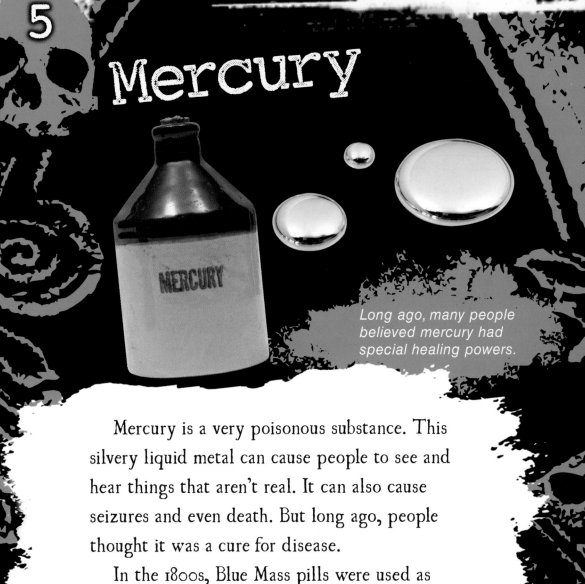

Long ago, many people believed mercury had special healing powers.

Mercury is a very poisonous substance. This silvery liquid metal can cause people to see and hear things that aren't real. It can also cause seizures and even death. But long ago, people thought it was a cure for disease.

In the 1800s, Blue Mass pills were used as a cure for many illnesses. The blue medicine contained large amounts of mercury. Just one dose was extremely dangerous by today's standards. It also had lots of licorice and honey to cover up the terrible taste. Blue Mass was very popular. Even Abraham Lincoln used Blue Mass pills before he became president!

MERCURY AND MUSHROOMS

China's first emperor, Qin Shi Huang Ti, was obsessed with living forever. He promised rich rewards for anyone who could help him cheat death.

One day, a magician claimed he had discovered the answer. He said a special mushroom grew on a distant island. He made a potion from the mushroom and claimed that it could defeat death. The emperor insisted on drinking the mushroom potion so he could live forever. Unfortunately, it contained large amounts of mercury. Instead of giving the emperor everlasting life, the potion killed him.

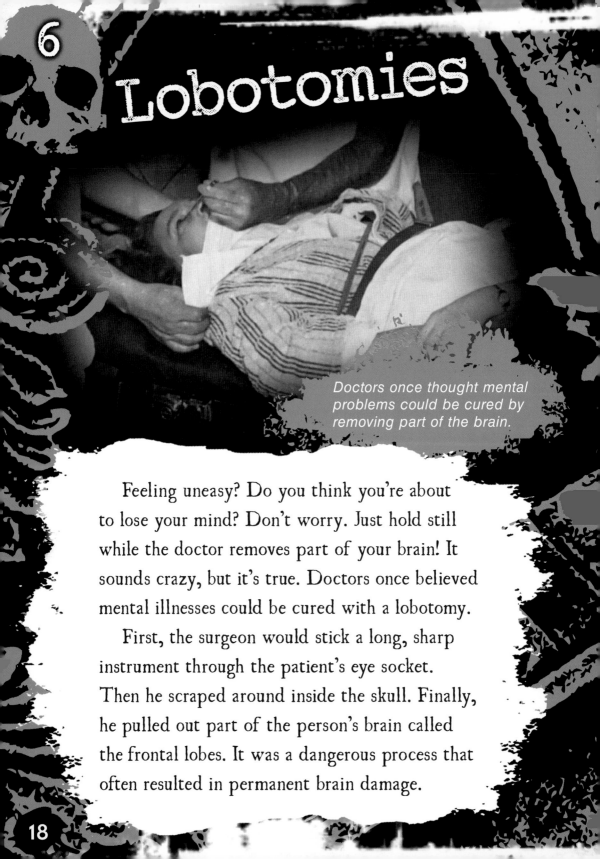

6

Lobotomies

Doctors once thought mental problems could be cured by removing part of the brain.

Feeling uneasy? Do you think you're about to lose your mind? Don't worry. Just hold still while the doctor removes part of your brain! It sounds crazy, but it's true. Doctors once believed mental illnesses could be cured with a lobotomy.

First, the surgeon would stick a long, sharp instrument through the patient's eye socket. Then he scraped around inside the skull. Finally, he pulled out part of the person's brain called the frontal lobes. It was a dangerous process that often resulted in permanent brain damage.

It's no surprise that many people died from lobotomies. Those who survived often lost the ability to think, speak, or use the bathroom. Thankfully, mental illness is now treated with medicine instead of dangerous brain surgery.

MESSING WITH THE MIND

There are many examples of people who were given lobotomies against their will. In 1960, Howard Dully was given a lobotomy as a boy. His stepmother didn't like his bad behavior. She brought Howard to the doctor but didn't tell him what was about to happen. She just told him to behave. Dully had no memory of the operation. He didn't learn about it until he was an adult. When he discovered it he said, "I always felt different — wondered if something's missing from my soul."

7

Cruel Mental Treatments

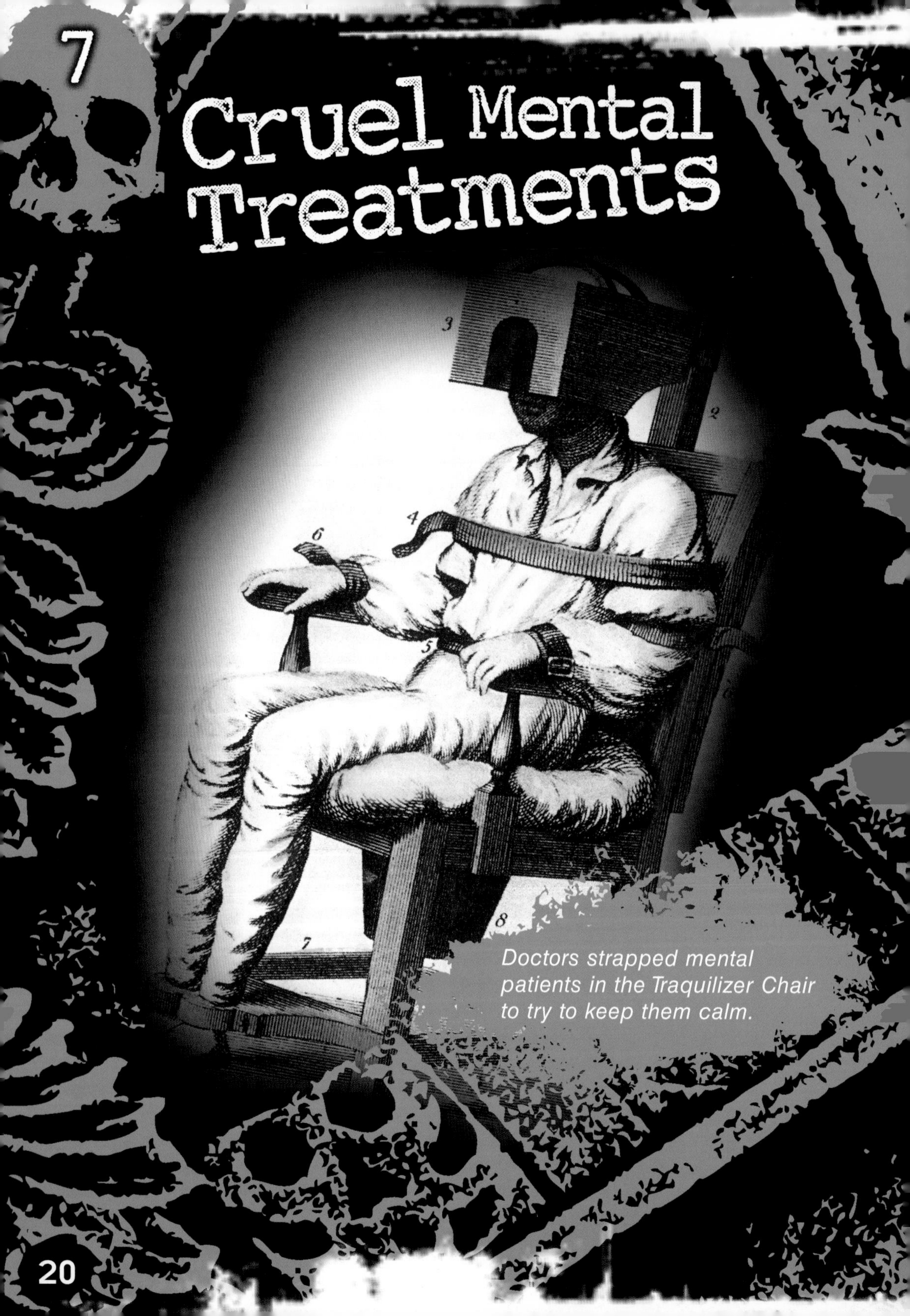
3
2
4
6
5
8
7

Doctors strapped mental patients in the Traquilizer Chair to try to keep them calm.

Long ago, people feared those with mental illnesses. Mentally ill people were often believed to be witches or possessed by demons. They were often thrown in jail or even put to death.

Eventually, doctors learned that mental illnesses involved a person's brain. Doctors decided that special hospitals were needed for mental patients. Unfortunately, many of the **treatments** used in these hospitals were cruel.

One popular treatment for mental patients was the Tranquilizer Chair. Patients were tightly strapped into a chair so they couldn't move. Then a box was placed over their heads. The box was stuffed with cloth so they couldn't turn their heads. The cloth also kept them from seeing or hearing anything. Doctors thought that complete stillness and silence helped calm patients. It was rarely effective, however.

treatment — a process used to heal a wound or cure an illness

The Wooden Crib, or restraining bed, was another cruel device. Patients were tightly strapped into a bed that looked like a baby's crib. They were forced to lie still for up to 18 hours a day. They weren't even allowed to go to the bathroom. Patients were often left in the beds for days at a time. Nobody bothered to check on them or give them any food or water.

In the late 1700s, Dr. Johan Reil developed a truly crazy treatment. A patient was placed inside a large, hollow wooden wheel. Then the patient was forced to run for 36 straight hours. Dr. Reil thought his treatment helped patients behave properly. But perhaps they were just too tired to cause any problems!

HORRIBLE FACT

Other early treatments for mental illness included bloodletting and trepanations. Some doctors even dunked their patients in icy cold water!

THE SPIN DOCTOR

In the early 1800s, Dr. Benjamin Rush invented a new treatment for mental illness. He strapped his patients into a chair hanging in midair. Then he spun them in circles for hours at a time.

The patients often vomited, which Rush thought was helpful. He thought vomiting helped get rid of whatever made them sick. However, the spinning treatment didn't really work. Rush only made his patients really dizzy!

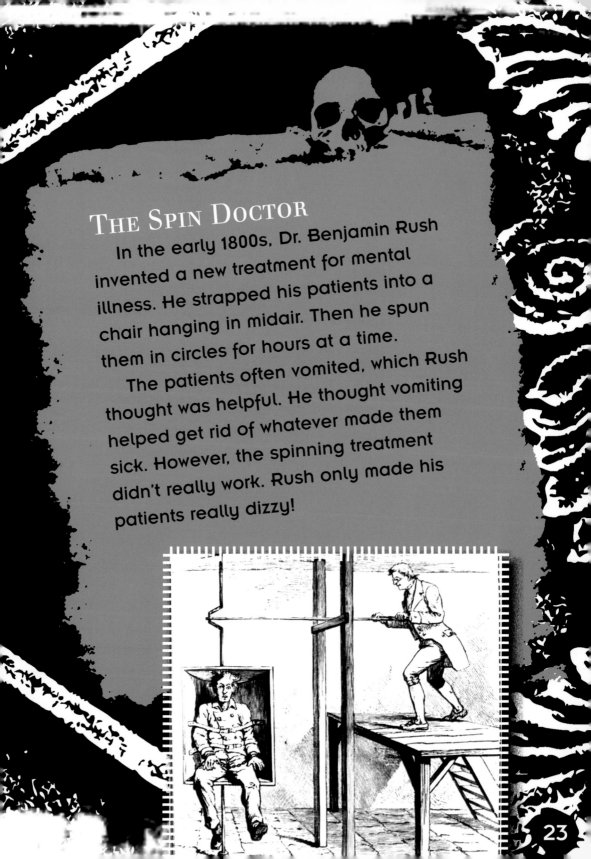

The Vibratory Chair

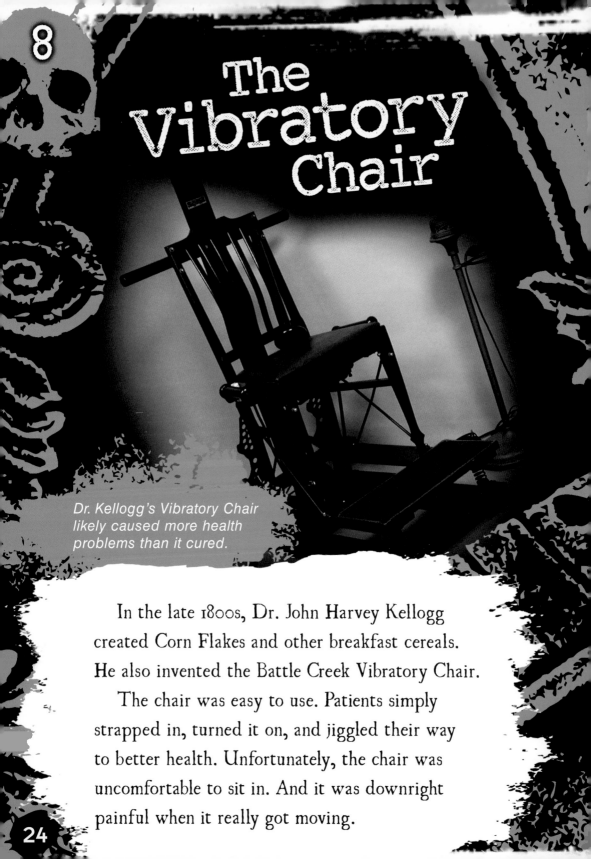

Dr. Kellogg's Vibratory Chair likely caused more health problems than it cured.

In the late 1800s, Dr. John Harvey Kellogg created Corn Flakes and other breakfast cereals. He also invented the Battle Creek Vibratory Chair.

The chair was easy to use. Patients simply strapped in, turned it on, and jiggled their way to better health. Unfortunately, the chair was uncomfortable to sit in. And it was downright painful when it really got moving.

But Dr. Kellogg insisted that his chair could relieve almost any health problem. He thought the chair helped restore the proper balance of **bacteria** in people's bodies. Just a few minutes in the chair would supposedly help relieve digestive problems. A little longer, and patients could be cured of headaches and backaches.

bacteria — microscopic living organisms that can cause disease

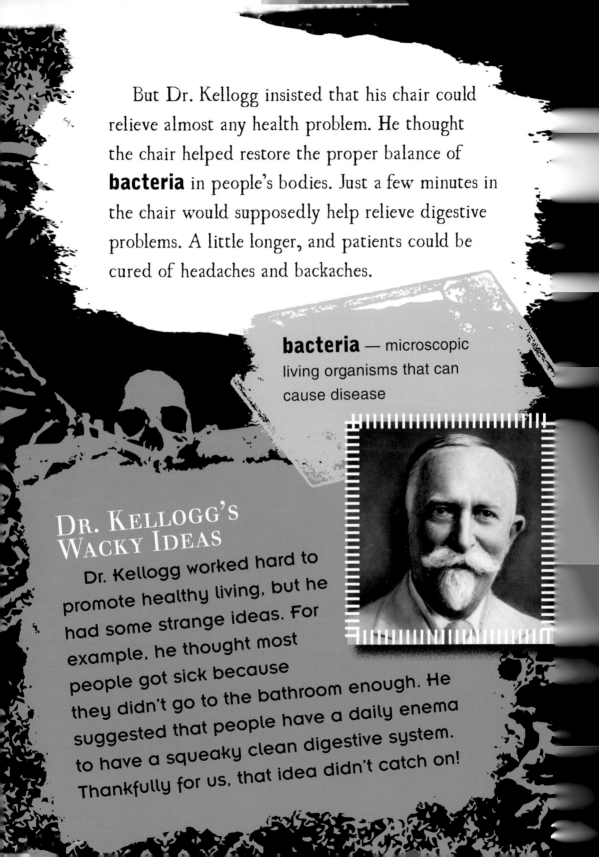

Dr. Kellogg's Wacky Ideas

Dr. Kellogg worked hard to promote healthy living, but he had some strange ideas. For example, he thought most people got sick because they didn't go to the bathroom enough. He suggested that people have a daily enema to have a squeaky clean digestive system. Thankfully for us, that idea didn't catch on!

Magnets to the Rescue

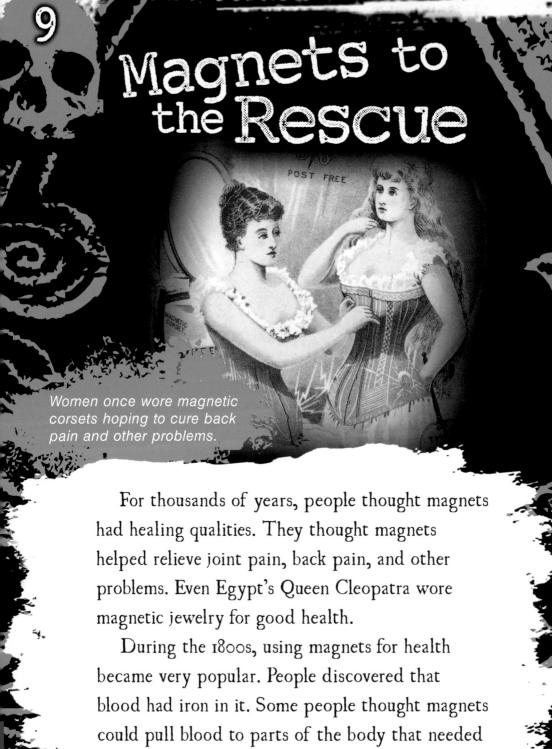

POST FREE

MAGNETIC CORSET.

Women once wore magnetic corsets hoping to cure back pain and other problems.

For thousands of years, people thought magnets had healing qualities. They thought magnets helped relieve joint pain, back pain, and other problems. Even Egypt's Queen Cleopatra wore magnetic jewelry for good health.

During the 1800s, using magnets for health became very popular. People discovered that blood had iron in it. Some people thought magnets could pull blood to parts of the body that needed healing. Companies sold many magnetic items like belts, hats, shoes, and boots.

Luckily, the iron in our blood isn't metallic at all. If it was, doctors couldn't use a method called Magnetic Resonance Imaging (MRI) to scan the inside of the body. An MRI machine is so strong that it can pull metal objects with the speed of a bullet. If people had metallic blood, the machine would pull it right out of their bodies!

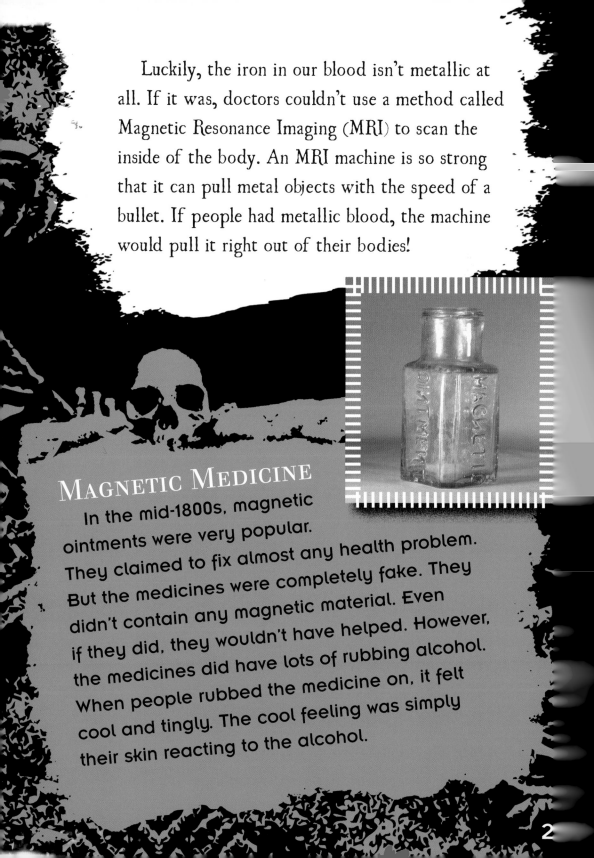

MAGNETIC MEDICINE

In the mid-1800s, magnetic ointments were very popular. They claimed to fix almost any health problem. But the medicines were completely fake. They didn't contain any magnetic material. Even if they did, they wouldn't have helped. However, the medicines did have lots of rubbing alcohol. When people rubbed the medicine on, it felt cool and tingly. The cool feeling was simply their skin reacting to the alcohol.

See it up Close

Want to see some of the disturbing medical tools of the past? Head to the Science Museum in St. Paul, Minnesota. Inside, you'll find the Questionable Medical Devices exhibit. It has several of the crazy machines people once used to make their lives better.

While there, you can see the MacGregor Rejuvenator. This strange machine was thought to reverse the aging process. It used magnets, radio waves, and dangerous levels of ultraviolet light. Too much ultraviolet light can cause sunburn, wrinkles, and skin cancer. Instead of making people look younger, it made them look older!

Today's doctors use only the best treatments for their patients. There's no reason to be afraid the next time you visit the doctor. But long ago, visiting the doctor's office could be a truly frightening — and deadly — experience.

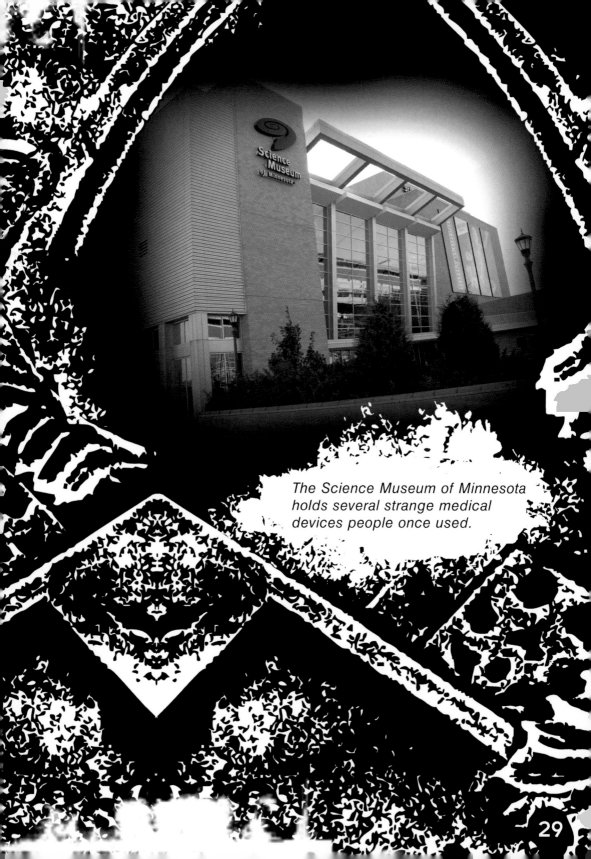

The Science Museum of Minnesota holds several strange medical devices people once used.

Glossary

addiction (uh-DIK-shun) — a dependence on a drug or other substance

artery (AR-tuh-ree) — a blood vessel that carries blood away from the heart

bacteria (bak-TEER-ee-uh) — microscopic living organisms that can cause disease

enema (EN-uh-muh) — an injection of fluid that causes a bowel movement

seizure (SEE-zhur) — a sudden attack of violent spasms in a person's body

surgery (SUR-jer-ee) — an operation to repair or remove damaged body parts

telepathic (tel-uh-PATH-ik) — the ability to read minds

treatment (TREET-muhnt) — a process used to heal a wound or cure an illness

Read More

Goldsmith, Connie. *Cutting-Edge Medicine.* Cool Science. Minneapolis: Lerner, 2008.

Strom, Laura Layton. *Dr. Medieval: Medicine in the Middle Ages.* Shockwave Science. New York: Children's Press, 2008.

Williams, Dinah. *Abandoned Insane Asylums.* Scary Places. New York: Bearport, 2008.

Internet Sites

FactHound offers a safe, fun way to find educator-approved Internet sites related to this book.

Here's what you do:

1. Visit *www.facthound.com*
2. Choose your grade level.
3. Begin your search.

This book's ID number is 9781429622936.

FactHound will fetch the best sites for you!

Index